Horses
of the Sea

PAGE PUBLISHING, INC.
New York, NY

First originally published by Page Publishing, Inc. 2017

ISBN 978-1-64082-751-6 (Paperback)
ISBN 978-1-64082-753-0 (Hardcover)
ISBN 978-1-64082-752-3 (Digital)

Printed in the United States of America

Horses

of the Sea

To: Avery Grattan,
I love that you love reading and am
proud to have my book in your collection.
Thank you Avery for inviting me to your school!
It is a dream come true for me! XOXO
Pat Gleichauf
3-5-18

by

Patricia Gleichauf

Illustrated by

Shari Holcomb

To David and Daniel,
your curiosity is my inspiration.
Xoxo.

Horses of the sea
are not like horses of the land,

1

they cannot run
like ponies across the sand.

2

They live in salt water,
they play in the sea,

not on the beach
like you and me.

They have a long snout
that they use to eat.

They mostly eat fish,
they never eat meat.

They each have a unique crown
upon their head,

that matches their color—
yellow, green, blue, or red.

A seahorse can change color for many reasons,
even for the change of seasons.

They often change color
when danger is near,

to hide among sea plants
until the coast is clear.

Their eyes can see all around,
side to side,
up and down.

12

Their fins move very fast,
but seahorses move as slow as snails.
When they want to stand still, they
hang on with their tails.

They have fins on their head that look like ears,
that help them to swim, not to hear.

On their backs, they have a dorsal fin,
that pushes them forward so they don't spin.

If the dorsal fin should get torn,

it will grow back to
look like the day they
were born.

Some are spotted,
some have stripes.

There are many different types.

Seahorses sleep standing upright.
They just close their eyes and say, "Good night!"

Horses of the sea
are wonderful creatures.

They are beautiful fish
with magical features!

ABOUT THE AUTHOR

Pat (Anthony) Gleichauf has been caring for, raising, teaching, and writing for children of all ages most of her adult life. She has recently retired from a career in nursing that ranged from pediatrics to clinical research. In her retirement, Pat is able to devote more time to writing. Although she has had several children's stories published in magazines, this is her first children's book. Pat lives in Upstate New York with her husband, Jack. She has five grandchildren, who are perfect *story-testers*!

ABOUT THE ILLUSTRATOR

Shari (Knight, Williams) Holcomb grew up in Gladwin Michigan. After high school, she moved to Palmer, Alaska where she married, raised a daughter and resided for thirty two years. During that time, she completed a BSA in drawing from the University of Alaska, and later an MA in art history from Savannah College of Art and Design in Georgia. Shari taught art in the Alaska college system and in her studio for many years. Returning to Michigan in 2005, she taught at Mid Michigan Community College. Now remarried and retired, Shari spends summers in Gladwin and winters in Venice, Florida.

CPSIA information can be obtained
at www.ICGtesting.com
Printed in the USA
BVOW05s0300301217
504055BV00003B/5/P